NATURAL DISASTERS

Volcanoes

by Betsy Rathburn

BELLWETHER MEDIA • MINNEAPOLIS, MN

Note to Librarians, Teachers, and Parents:

Blastoff! Readers are carefully developed by literacy experts and combine standards-based content with developmentally appropriate text.

Level 1 provides the most support through repetition of high-frequency words, light text, predictable sentence patterns, and strong visual support.

Level 2 offers early readers a bit more challenge through varied simple sentences, increased text load, and less repetition of high-frequency words.

Level 3 advances early-fluent readers toward fluency through increased text and concept load, less reliance on visuals, longer sentences, and more literary language.

Level 4 builds reading stamina by providing more text per page, increased use of punctuation, greater variation in sentence patterns, and increasingly challenging vocabulary.

Level 5 encourages children to move from "learning to read" to "reading to learn" by providing even more text, varied writing styles, and less familiar topics.

Whichever book is right for your reader, Blastoff! Readers are the perfect books to build confidence and encourage a love of reading that will last a lifetime!

This edition first published in 2020 by Bellwether Media, Inc.

No part of this publication may be reproduced in whole or in part without written permission of the publisher. For information regarding permission, write to Bellwether Media, Inc., Attention: Permissions Department, 6012 Blue Circle Drive, Minnetonka, MN 55343.

Library of Congress Cataloging-in-Publication Data

Names: Rathburn, Betsy, author.
Title: Volcanoes / by Betsy Rathburn.
Description: Minneapolis, MN : Bellwether Media, Inc., [2020] | Series:
   Blastoff! Readers: Natural Disasters | Audience: Ages 5-8. | Audience: K
   to grade 3. | Includes bibliographical references and index.
Identifiers: LCCN 2019003809 (print) | LCCN 2019010904 (ebook) | ISBN
   9781618915702 (ebook) | ISBN 9781644870297 (hardcover : alk. paper) | ISBN
   9781618917508 (pbk. : alk. paper)
Subjects: LCSH: Volcanoes--Juvenile literature. | Natural disasters--Juvenile
   literature. | Emergency management--Juvenile literature.
Classification: LCC QE521.3 (ebook) | LCC QE521.3 .R3757 2020 (print) | DDC 551.21--dc23
LC record available at https://lccn.loc.gov/2019003809

Editor: Al Albertson   Designer: Josh Brink

Printed in the United States of America, North Mankato, MN

Table of **Contents**

What Are Volcanoes?

lava

erupting volcano

Volcanoes are **vents** in the earth's crust. They come in many forms. They may look like steep mountains or round hills.

Volcanoes are found in certain places around the world. Sometimes, they **erupt**! They shoot out hot ash and **lava**.

Major Active Volcanoes

active volcano = 🌋

N
W — E
S

How Do Volcanoes Form?

Volcanoes come from **magma**. This hot, melted rock gathers in underground **magma chambers**.

Magma is lighter than solid rock. **Pressure** helps it rise through layers of rock.

How Volcanoes Erupt

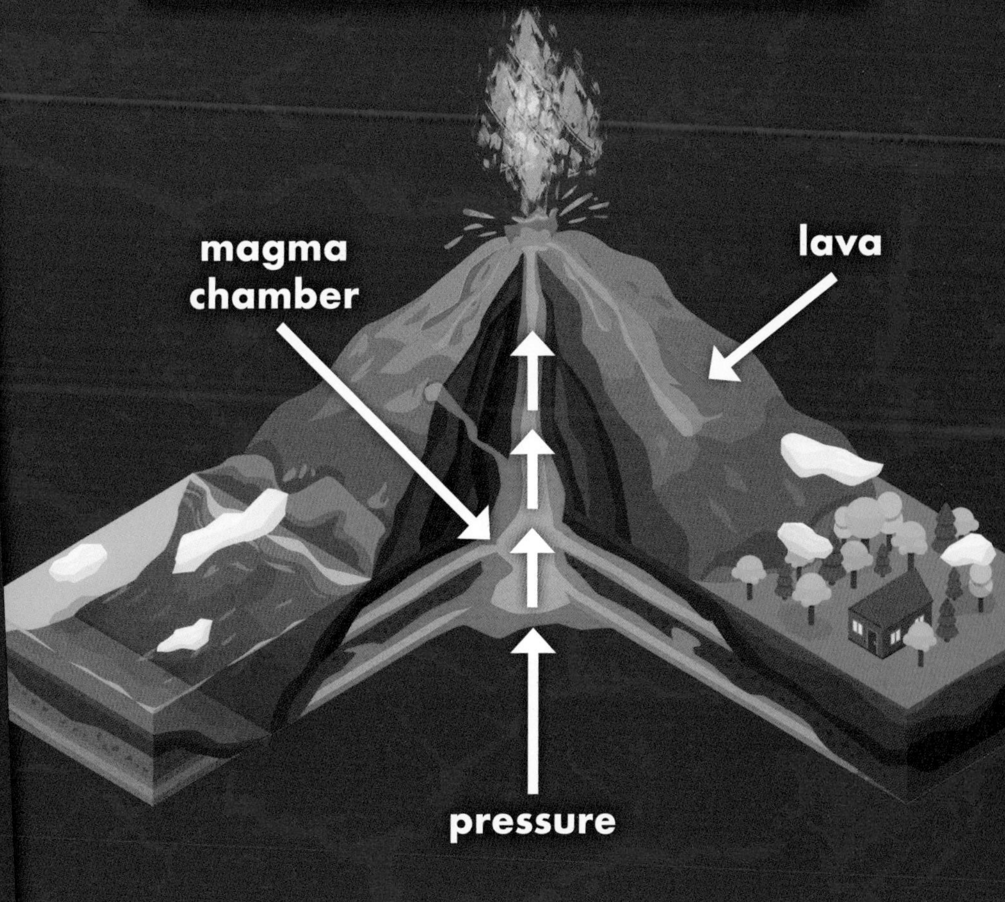

magma chamber

lava

pressure

Over time, magma reaches the earth's surface. It erupts as lava!

Cooling lava creates layers of rock that grow over time. Many layers around a vent make a big volcano!

lava rock

Magma can be runny or sticky. Runny magma does not hold a lot of gas. It moves slowly when it reaches the earth's surface.

Sticky magma has more gas. It gets stuck inside the earth. The pressure builds into a powerful blast!

Volcano Damage

plume

Some eruptions shoot **plumes** of ash and lava high into the air. Nearby people and buildings are in danger!

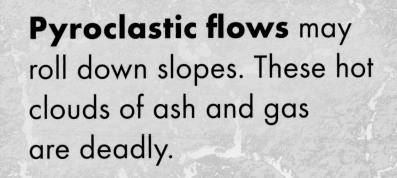

Pyroclastic flows may roll down slopes. These hot clouds of ash and gas are deadly.

pyroclastic flow

Ash is unsafe to breathe. It may harm eyes and skin. It can **pollute** drinking water.

We measure how often small and big eruptions happen. The **Volcanic Explosivity Index** helps us compare.

volcanic ash

Volcanic Explosivity Index

	Plume Height	How Often?
0	less than 328 feet (100 meters)	continuous
1	328 to 3,281 feet (100 to 1,000 meters)	daily
2	0.6 to 3 miles (1 to 5 kilometers)	weekly
3	2 to 9 miles (3 to 15 kilometers)	every few months
4	6 to 16 miles (10 to 25 kilometers)	about once every year
5	12 to 22 miles (20 to 35 kilometers)	about once every 10 years
6	more than 19 miles (30 kilometers)	about once every 100 years
7	more than 25 miles (40 kilometers)	about once every 1,000 years
8	more than 31 miles (50 kilometers)	about once every 10,000 years

Lava can reach more than 2,000 degrees Fahrenheit (1,093 degrees Celsius). It ruins everything in its path.

Slow-moving lava spreads across roads and yards. Roads and houses may be destroyed. It may take years to rebuild after the disaster.

Predicting Disaster

Past information can help **predict** future eruptions. It tells scientists when a volcano might explode.

Seismometers also help predict disaster. They measure earthquakes that can lead to eruptions.

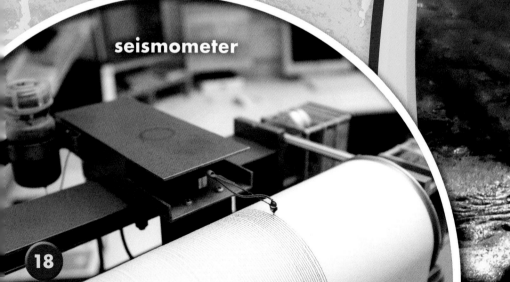

seismometer

18

Volcanic Eruption Profile

Name: 2018 Kilauea eruption

Dates: May 3, 2018 to September 4, 2018

Location: Hawaii

Damage to Property:
- more than 700 homes destroyed
- $28 million in damage to farms
- up to $800 million in damage overall

Damage to People:
- at least 2,500 people evacuated
- hundreds of people lost homes
- long-lasting injuries from breathing volcanic ash

2018 Kilauea eruption

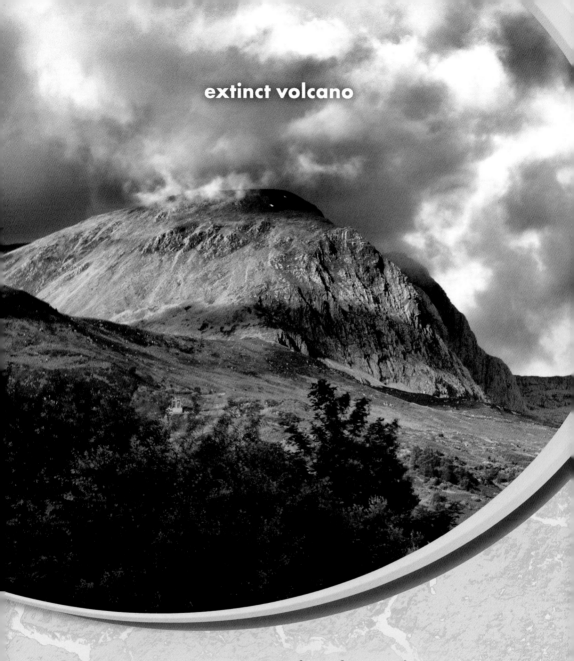

extinct volcano

Scientists consider how long volcanoes are **dormant**. Some may erupt again one day. Others will go **extinct**.

Eruptions cannot be prevented. People near volcanoes must watch for signs of disaster. They may need to **evacuate**!

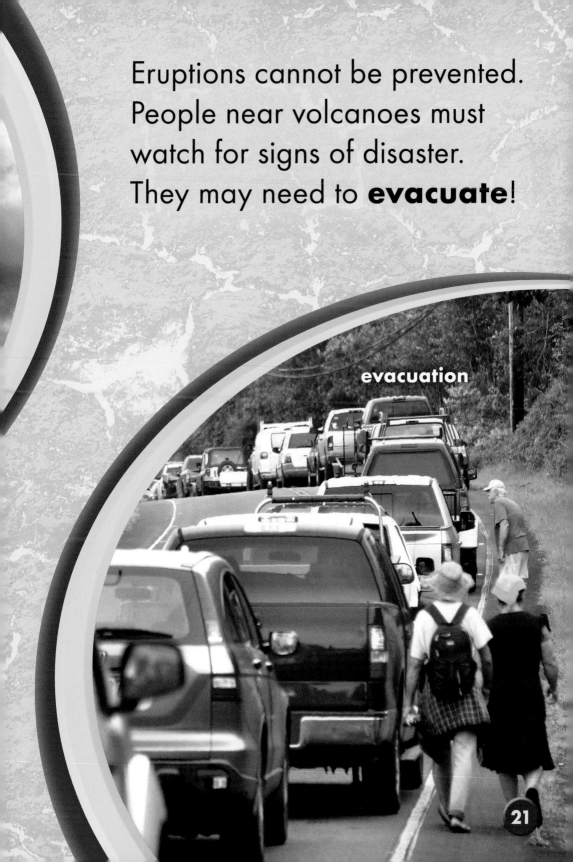

evacuation

Glossary

dormant—active but not currently erupting; dormant volcanoes are expected to erupt again.

erupt—to force out lava and ash

evacuate—to leave a dangerous area

extinct—no longer active

lava—magma that reaches the earth's surface

magma—melted rock that forms underground

magma chambers—areas below the earth's surface where magma is stored

plumes—tall streams of ash, rock, magma, and other materials

pollute—to make dirty or unusable

predict—to guess based on collected data

pressure—a force that pushes against things

pyroclastic flows—hot ash, lava pieces, and gases shot out of a volcano that flow quickly down its slopes

seismometers—tools that measure earthquakes

vents—openings in the earth's crust from which magma can erupt

Volcanic Explosivity Index—a tool that compares the strength of volcanic eruptions and how often they occur

To Learn More

AT THE LIBRARY

Ganeri, Anita. *Eruption!: The Story of Volcanoes*. New York; N.Y.: DK Publishing, 2015.

Nargi, Lela, and Arianna Soldati. *Volcanoes*. Washington, D.C.: National Geographic, 2018.

Rathburn, Betsy. *Earthquakes*. Minneapolis, Minn.: Bellwether Media, 2020.

ON THE WEB

FACTSURFER

Factsurfer.com gives you a safe, fun way to find more information.

1. Go to www.factsurfer.com.

2. Enter "volcanoes" into the search box and click 🔍.

3. Select your book cover to see a list of related web sites.

Index

The images in this book are reproduced through the courtesy of: fboundrias, cover (hero); Willyam Bradberry, cover (lava); Yvonne Baurs, cover (rock); Ammit Jack, CIP; shayes17, p. 4; Puripat Lertpunyaroj, p. 6; Rvector, p. 7; Phil Degginger/ Alamy, p. 8; David Hayes/ Alamy, p. 10; Avanius, p. 11; Kirill Smirnov, p. 12; Sijori Images/ Alamy, p. 13; Barry Lewis/ Alamy, p. 14; himanshu shah, p. 15; Manfred Thürig/ Alamy, p. 16; FEMA/ Alamy, p. 17; Anton Luhr/ Newscom, p. 18; RGB Ventures/ Alamy, p. 19; Maaster, p. 20; Frederic J. Brown/ Getty Images, p. 21.